Provand's Lordship and Old Glasgow

Glasgow Museums

Text and photography copyright ©2004 Glasgow City Council (Museums)

First published in 2004 by Glasgow City Council (Museums)

ISBN 0 902752 75 8

Text by Helen Avenell
Edited by Bill Jenkins
Designed by Simon Gilmovitch

The publishers gratefully acknowledge T&R Annan & Sons Ltd for permission to reproduce the photographs on pages 53 and 61.

Special thanks are due to Dr Stephen Driscoll of Glasgow University for his comments and suggestions on the text, and for contributing a fitting foreword to this publication.

Photographs are from Glasgow City Council (Museums) Photo Library and Photography Department, unless otherwise acknowledged. Illustration on page 10 by Jeff Fallow

We would also like to thank all the staff and volunteers at Glasgow Museums whose hard work made this publication possible.

This guidebook owes much to previous literature written on Provand's Lordship, in particular, *The Oldest House in Glasgow*. Written by William Gemmell in 1910, and published in small numbers by the Provand's Lordship Society, this book has greatly informed the current publication.

www.glasgowmuseums.com

Contents

LET GLASGOW FLOURISH

ARMS OF THE CITY OF GLASGOW

NEMO ME IMPVNE LACESSIT

FOREWORD

Provand's Lordship is a remarkable building, yet its solid, undistinguished, exterior provides little hint of its historical significance. As this guide makes clear, Provand's Lordship is a unique treasure; it is genuinely representative of the past.

Like Glasgow itself, Provand's Lordship owes its existence to the great cathedral. The sturdy masonry, which made it such a functional building over the centuries, set Provand's Lordship apart from the commonplace dwellings of timber. The high-quality building materials and its spacious interiors testify to the wealth of the cathedral community; however Provand's Lordship is not simply a sign of elite patronage. The physical existence of this unique medieval building allows us to consider the social reality of the medieval city in a concrete way.

As the centre of power shifted away from the cathedral to the modern commercial city, so too Provand's Lordship was transformed. The changes in use and social status provide remarkable insights into life in the post-medieval city. No less revealing are the circumstances behind the acquisition of the building by industrial worthies and its elevation to an icon of civic pride. All these disparate historical strands running through Provand's Lordship make it more than just another old house. For the first time we have an accessible guide which brings out the historical significance of Provand's Lordship for Glasgow and Scotland.

Stephen T Driscoll
Department of Archaeology
University of Glasgow

INTRODUCTION

A visit to Provand's Lordship is a step into Glasgow's medieval past. With the exception of Glasgow Cathedral, Provand's Lordship is the city's oldest surviving building and dates from the end of the fifteenth century. It stands witness to Glasgow's illuminating, exciting, and sometimes troubled, past.

The city of Glasgow has a history stretching back over nearly 1,000 years. In the sixth century, St Kentigern, also known as St Mungo, established a Christian community on the banks of the Molendinar Burn and began the process of establishing a permanent settlement that would become known as Glasgow. St Mungo became the patron saint of Glasgow and his legacy lives on today in Glasgow's armorial bearings and motto. Following the death of St Mungo, a small wooden church was built over his burial place and a religious foundation developed. Little is known of the site until the twelfth century, but in 1136, records show that a stone church was blessed on the site of the present cathedral in the presence of King David I of Scotland.

From the twelfth century Glasgow grew in importance as a religious and ecclesiastical site and in 1175 the town was granted burgh status. The tomb of St Mungo became a place of pilgrimage, and as a result the cathedral was twice rebuilt with the addition of numerous shrines and altars to cater for the needs of the pilgrims. By the fifteenth

left
View of Glasgow and the cathedral from the north, mid-seventeenth century.

century, the streets and narrow passages near the cathedral saw the development of an ecclesiastical precinct of manses. Provand's Lordship was one of approximately 24 stone built dwellings built as lodgings for the clergy who served in the cathedral. In 1492, Robert Blacader became the first Archbishop of Glasgow, establishing Glasgow as a major ecclesiastical city in Scotland, second only in importance to St Andrews. As the city flourished, Glasgow grew into a bustling town and by 1670 the population was nearing 14,000 people.

In 1736, local man John McUre published *A View of the City of Glasgow*, the first history of the city. He wrote about it in glowing terms:

> The City is surrounded with Corn-fields, Kitchen and Flower-gardens, and beautiful orchyards, abounding with Fruits of all Sorts, which, by Reason of the large and open streets, send furth a pleasant and odiferous smell.

Glasgow's location on the west coast of Scotland made it the perfect site for trade with the New World, and throughout the seventeenth and eighteenth centuries the city became a progressive, enlightened and wealthy commercial centre. Provand's Lordship, having surrendered its religious connections following the Protestant Reformation, became home to a succession of commercial ventures including a tailor's workshop, an alehouse and later even a sweetshop.

By the early twentieth century, Provand's Lordship and Glasgow Cathedral were the sole surviving buildings of the medieval city. Most of Glasgow's medieval architecture had disappeared in successive demolition and building programmes supported by the City Improvement Trust in the nineteenth century. In 1906, Provand's Lordship was under threat from developers but was rescued by a group of interested Glasgow citizens who formed the Provand's Lordship Society. They successfully secured the long-term survival of the house for future generations. In 1979, the oldest house in Glasgow was gifted into the trusteeship of Glasgow Council.

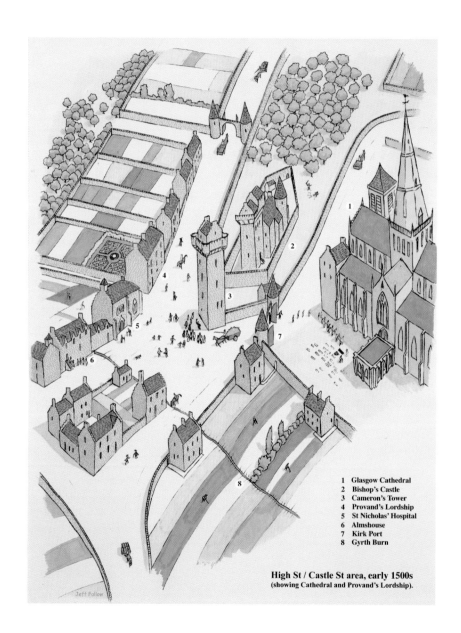

1   Glasgow Cathedral
2   Bishop's Castle
3   Cameron's Tower
4   Provand's Lordship
5   St Nicholas' Hospital
6   Almshouse
7   Kirk Port
8   Gyrth Burn

High St / Castle St area, early 1500s
(showing Cathedral and Provand's Lordship).

Jeff Follow

10

GLASGOW'S EARLY YEARS

The origins of Provand's Lordship

Provand's Lordship was built over 500 years ago, when the population of Glasgow was just a few thousand people and the focus of daily life centred on the cathedral.

Earliest records tell us that Provand's Lordship was constructed sometime around the year 1471 by Andrew Muirhead, Bishop of Glasgow, and his coat of arms, three acorns on a bend, can still be faintly seen cut into the lowest crow step on the southeast gable. It was built as the manse, or living quarters, for the priest of the Chapel and Hospital of St Nicholas, an almshouse established for the support of 12 elderly poor men.

The house originally consisted of nine separate, self-contained chambers, each with a fireplace in the south wall. The three chambers on ground level each had their own entrance but those on the middle and top floors were accessed by wooden stairs and balconies on the west side of the building. There was a large garden and orchard and each room had two windows looking eastward towards the cathedral and the bishop's castle, situated on the present-day site of Cathedral Square.

By the thirteenth century, Glasgow had developed from a small site of pilgrimage into a significant ecclesiastical

left
Artist's impression of the cathedral precinct, c.1500.

centre. As an archbishopric, the church had responsibility for a large geographical area and the cathedral had 32 clergymen, or canons. These men were nominated by the bishop and formed the cathedral chapter, serving in surrounding parishes and assisting with the administration of the diocese. Every year, the canons were required to spend roughly three months at the church in Glasgow, and while in service, most lived near to the cathedral. By 1430, it was clear that there were not enough lodgings to house these men and Bishop John Cameron began a building programme. He demanded that each canon should have a suitable residence in the town during his stay in Glasgow. Over the next 50 years, successive bishops added to Cameron's plans and the area around the cathedral precinct became a lively hub. Similar precincts can still be seen surrounding English cathedrals, for instance Wells Cathedral in Somerset.

What's in a name?

Although Provand's Lordship was built as part of St Nicholas' Hospital, its separate chambers made the building perfect for use as a shared housing complex. The house was put to use as temporary lodgings for cathedral clergy and one of the rooms became the official dwelling of the Prebendary of Barlanark. All the canons serving at Glasgow Cathedral were supported financially by their prebend, or living. This income usually came from church tithes, a church tax collected from the local people in their home parish. The prebend of Barlanark was slightly different, as money

Andrew Muirhead

Bishop Andrew Muirhead was the founder of Provand's Lordship. He came from the family of Muirheads of Lauchop, one of the ancient shires of Lanark. He was consecrated as bishop in 1455 and during his 18-year term he was responsible for some of Glasgow's finest medieval buildings.

A student of St Andrews and Paris and a visitor to Rome, Bishop Andrew was a cultured man who influenced the development of the University of Glasgow in its early years. As well as building St Nicholas' Hospital and Manse, he established an official choir. Traditionally, music and song in the cathedral was led by a nominated canon known as a chanter or precentor, but these men were often not particularly

Seal of Bishop Andrew Muirhead, 1455–73.

gifted as singers and Muirhead decided that a trained choir would be more fitting for the growing cathedral community. He established the Vicars Choral; 12 priests who were formally trained in singing and who resided together in a specially built house just north of the cathedral. The most tangible evidence of Bishop Andrew Muirhead's patronage is a commemoration stone inscribed as follows:

Has pater Andreas antistes condidit edes
Presbiteris choro Glasgu famulantibus almo.
(These buildings Bishop Andrew put up
for the priests who serve the flourishing
choir of Glasgow.)

This stone is now displayed in Provand's Lordship and can be seen in the mid-chamber on the ground floor.

Vicars Choral Stone, commemorating the patronage of Bishop Andrew Muirhead.

Bishop Andrew Muirhead died in November 1473 at his palace opposite Provand's Lordship. He was laid to rest in the choir of the cathedral church.

was not raised from gathering church taxes but solely from the rental of land known as the estate of Provan. The territory of Provan consisted of about 800 hectares (2,000 acres) of land lying to the east of Glasgow. The Church gave the holder of this prebend wide-ranging power and the canon became known as the Lord of Provan. The townhouse in Glasgow became known as Provand's Lordship, a name used by historians frequently in the nineteenth century. Provan Hall, the country residence of the old prebend of Provan dates from the sixteenth century and also survives, although it is now enveloped in the post-war housing estate of Garthamlock in the east of Glasgow.

Although Provand's Lordship looks small to modern eyes, it would have been regarded as a handsome and important building in the fifteenth century. It is sometimes assumed that life for the clergy in such manses was cold, spartan and colourless but a surviving inventory from the Stobo Manse in Drygate, dated 1542, shows a very different situation. This extremely rare register shows that the resident priest had a wardrobe of luxurious clothes trimmed with fur and a great deal of expensive furniture. Items such as Flemish tapestries, armour and hunting gear are also listed and would not have been out of place in a noble's household. Smaller valuables included a rosary with beads made from gold coins and even a silver toothpick.

left
Façade of Provan Hall,
Garthamlock.

Alms House.   S. Nicholas'   Bp. Cameron's Tower.   Lord Darnley
                  Hospital and Chapel.   Cottage.

The Hospital of St Nicholas

Caring for the poor and less fortunate was one of the principal responsibilities of the bishop, and the building of St Nicholas' Hospital and Manse was part of the social welfare programme of its time. Although the foundation deeds of the hospital and chapel no longer exist, measurements and maps of old Glasgow show that the buildings were immediately south of Provand's Lordship, where Macleod Street and the Barony Church now stand.

The inmates of St Nicholas' Hospital were expected to wear white and to lead pious, almost monastic, lives. Inmates were paid a monthly allowance, and were given a new cloth gown every third year, and a pair of double-soled shoes every New Year. Bedding, coal and candles were provided and the men were required to pledge not to sell any of their belongings. Most days were spent in prayer or at work in the gardens and orchards, and those who did not abide by the rules were asked to leave.

The medieval city of Glasgow

Life in medieval Glasgow revolved around the church, and the principal building in the city was the cathedral. Dedicated to St Kentigern, Glasgow Cathedral was constructed and developed over several centuries.

Next in importance was the bishop's palace, the main residence of the bishop. The bishop had secular as well as spiritual responsibility for the burgh of Glasgow and managed the fairs and markets.

left
Woodcut showing the Great Tower of the bishop's castle, Darnley's Cottage, Glasgow Cathedral and St Nicholas' Chapel and Hospital on the left.

In addition, all financial and legal work in the burgh was
undertaken on behalf of the bishop. We know from the
results of archaeological digs that the bishop's residence
started life as a modest stone tower or keep, surrounded
by a moat and built as a protective retreat. Bishop
Cameron extended his home in the fifteenth century,
around the time of the building of Provand's Lordship,
and constructed a splendid square tower on the southern
wall. When Glasgow became an archbishopric in 1492,
the bishop's court was given responsibility for the affairs
of the counties of Argyll, Dunblane, Dunkeld and Galloway.
This meant increased wealth and status for the cathedral
and the new archbishop, and by the year 1530 the bishop's
palace had been transformed into a castle of magnificent
proportions. A wall over 4.5 metres (15 feet) high
enclosed five large circular towers and a gate house at
the southeastern corner formed the main entrance to
the grounds.

Clustered around the cathedral and bishop's castle were many manses similar to Provand's Lordship. These included the living quarters of the canons and the smaller houses of the vicars, who acted as deputies. These stone-built manses gave this part of the town, the Townhead, a character distinct from that of the lower town where the houses of the artisans were timber framed or wattle and daub, and less well built. Each manse had its own garden or orchard and the small streams of the Molendinar and Gyrth flowed through the precinct area towards the River Clyde.

It is impossible now to imagine what this bustling area looked like in the sixteenth century but a glance from the eastern windows of Provand's Lordship would have revealed a view out onto Castle Street, known in past times as the King's Highway, and the main thoroughfare into the town of Glasgow. Beyond the bishop's castle and the manse of Erskine was the residence of the Rector of Glasgow and the imposing cathedral. Looking down the High Street towards Glasgow Cross was a vibrant and lively townscape. The rough streets were fronted by tenements and booths, with backlands containing gardens and outhouses. Sometime in the thirteenth century, the small town reached the river and the first wooden bridge was built over the River Clyde. However, Glasgow remained small and only consisted of the main High Street with two crossroads, and its population stood at less than 2,000 inhabitants.

20

'The Way, the Truth, the Life': A university for Glasgow

On Trinity Sunday, 30 June 1451, an unusual public announcement was made from the Mercat Cross, at the foot of the High Street. The assembled townspeople were told that Pope Nicholas V had issued a Papal Bull of Foundation to establish a university in Glasgow. The charter stated that this new place of study should be modelled on the University of Bologna, with a faculty of Arts through which all students should progress before entering one of the higher faculties of Divinity, Law or Medicine for professional training. It was to be only the fourth university to be founded in the British Isles, and in Scotland, younger only than St Andrews.

Initially, the classes of this infant university were held in the cathedral and in a small tenement in Rotten Row, a street lying just south of Provand's Lordship. The building became known as the pedagogium or 'Auld Pedagogy', from the Greek *paedagogia*, meaning the practice of teaching. This building fell into disrepair when a new college was built on the High Street in the 1650s. The teachers at the university were clergymen, training others for the service of the church and although the university remained small by modern standards for several centuries, the presence of men of letters helped to put Glasgow's name on the European map.

left
Auld Pedagogy. Rented for living quarters and classes by the University of Glasgow in the late fifteenth century.

22

THE REFORMATION AND BEYOND

By the sixteenth century, Glasgow had become the second ecclesiastical city in Scotland. The city was a 'bishop's burgh', a privileged town which enjoyed the right to hold markets and participate in foreign trade. As in the rest of the country, the Church controlled all aspects of daily life from health to education, and religion played a central role in the lives of the population. It was clear, therefore, that the religious debates that led to the Reformation would have a significant effect on Glasgow. In 1560, John Knox, a Protestant reformer, led the movement that swept away the power of the existing Catholic Church and embraced a new Protestantism.

The effects of these cataclysmic events soon reached the steps of the cathedral in Glasgow. The army of the reforming Protestant lords, the Earls of Moray and Argyll and Lord Ruthven, overran the cathedral and bishop's castle. Archbishop James Beaton, who was to be Glasgow's last Catholic bishop, was forced to flee to France carrying with him the many jewels, relics and records of the archbishopric. Much of the original stained glass and images of the medieval church fell victim to the reformers' rejection of the use of paintings, imagery and lavish ornamentation. On 12 August 1560, instructions were dispatched throughout the kingdom by John Knox to cleanse the altars of the iconography of Catholicism and to 'purge the kirks of all kind of monuments of idolatrye'.

left
Defence of the Cathedral by the Trades' House in 1579 during the Reformation, by David Roberts (1796–1863).

Lord Henry Darnley.

Mary, Queen of Scots, as a young woman.
Copy of a painting by Czortonschi.

Mary, Queen of Scots, and the casket letters

One raw and bitter day in January 1567 Lord Henry Darnley, second husband of Mary, Queen of Scots, staggered into Glasgow from Stirling suffering from suspected smallpox. Generally disliked by the Royal Court for his belligerent manner and merciless ambition, and on bad terms with almost everyone, including his wife, he left Edinburgh and travelled to Glasgow, the home of his father the Earl of Lennox.

Mary herself was under attack from many quarters, not least as a Catholic queen in a country facing the religious upheaval of the Reformation. The treacherous politics of the Scottish court and the Protestant lords, including her half brother the Earl of Moray, threatened her very existence as queen.

Mary travelled to Glasgow to persuade her ill husband to come back to Edinburgh with her. She may have lodged at Provand's Lordship, owned by one of her advisors, William Baillie, Lord of Provan. Darnley returned to Edinburgh, but the following day he was killed in an explosion, believed by many to have been planned with Mary's help. Just three months later she married for the third time, to the Protestant Earl of Bothwell. Mary's enemies produced evidence in the form of the 'Casket Letters', a series of love letters and sonnets, supposedly written by Mary to Bothwell in 1566 and 1567. Controversy still surrounds the 'Casket Letters', but if they are genuine the most incriminating sections may have been written at Provand's Lordship. The 'Glasgow Letter' not only suggests Mary had a liaison with Bothwell but also that she was party to the murder of her husband.

Following the disastrous Battle of Langside in 1568, Mary was forced to abdicate and eventually fled to seek sanctuary with her cousin, Queen Elizabeth I of England. She spent the last 19 years of her life in captivity and was finally executed at Fotheringay Castle on 8 February 1587. Provand's Lordship may have played its part in the dramatic and tragic life of Mary, Queen of Scots.

However, many were not satisfied that the marks of Catholicism had been sufficiently removed and 14 years later, an act was passed sanctioning the demolition of any church that had not complied with the removal of idolatrous symbols. Andrew Melville, then Principal of Glasgow University, enthusiastically called for the flattening of the cathedral and the building of three new, more virtuous, churches. But he did not reckon on the craft guilds, who enjoyed the ownership of parts of the church nave and who regarded it as their own. It was made clear to Melville that any attempt to destroy the church would lead to serious consequences for him and his ministers. Ultimately, King James VI realized the possible cost of civil disorder, and the defence of the cathedral was secured. Today, thanks to the artisans of the ancient craft guilds, Glasgow Cathedral remains the only complete medieval cathedral on the Scottish mainland, the only other survivor being St Magnus Cathedral in Orkney.

New residents

With the withdrawal of Archbishop Beaton in 1560, the government of the archdiocese of Glasgow came to a standstill and chaos reigned in the city. The cathedral was closed for a time and the manses of many of the prebendaries were deserted or sold to private owners.

In 1560, the Prebendary of Balernock, like Provan, was held by Canon William Baillie. William Baillie was aware that the disruption caused by the Reformation would lead to abolition of the system of prebendaries, resulting in the loss of the title and property bestowed on him by the Old Church. In 1562, he appealed for permission to retain the estate of Provan and Provand's Lordship for his family, and eventually, in 1593, King James VI granted a charter naming William Baillie as the owner of the estate lands.

Provand's Lordship became the townhouse of the Baillies of Provand and when William Baillie died on 26 May 1593, the chain that linked the house to its ecclesiastical origins was broken. Provand's Lordship was left to Baillie's two sons, William and John, but neither had any children of their own, and so the house and lands of Provan estate went to William's daughter Elizabeth. In due course her eldest son Francis inherited the estate of Provan with the house at Townhead. Francis and his descendants proved to be spendthrifts and by 1667, the house and lands were sold to the City of Glasgow for 106,000 merks.

The earliest deed belonging to the house dates from 17 October 1642 and relates to the transfer of ownership to a John Trumbill and his wife Marion Finniesone. They did not keep the house for long, and within a year they passed it on to a tailor named William Bryson. A man of considerable means, Bryson added an extension to the

west side of the tenement, creating an internal stairway. The stone sundial that can be seen on the south gable of the house bears his initials 'WB' and the date 1670. William Bryson presents a fine figure of his time. As a successful businessman and property owner, he was characteristic of what was happening elsewhere in Glasgow at the time. The town was expanding rapidly and developing into a hub of commerce and enterprise.

The expanding city

Since the twelfth century, Glasgow had been evolving into almost two towns. On the hill stood the cathedral and the ecclesiastical centre of the town, while down the High Street towards the Trongate and Saltmarket, Glasgow's mercantile centre expanded. The principal building in the city after the cathedral and bishop's castle was the university. In 1460, the university moved to a purpose-built site at the bottom of the High Street. The area was enhanced in the 1650s by the construction of fine new college buildings, leading to the university being hailed as the most magnificent structure in the city.

Further down the High Street, Glasgow Cross represented the main intersection of the four original streets of the city. In 1626, this spot was marked by the erection of the Tolbooth, which housed the council house, courthouse and prison. Today, the steeple remains as the only relic of the original building and is one of only three original medieval

left
St Nicholas Garden and the west façade of Provand's Lordship, showing the extension added by William Bryson in 1670.

crowned steeples in the country. Entry to the prison wards was by a narrow turnpike stair in the Steeple, guarded by a janitor. Prisoners were held on the top floor of the Tolbooth and it was commonplace for debtors to lower a shoe by a cord from the upper windows down to the pavement in order to get coppers from sympathetic passers-by.

South of Glasgow Cross, the Saltmarket extended to the fording place on the banks of the River Clyde and was the residence of many of the magnates and merchants of the city in the seventeenth century. Bridgegate, or Briggait as it has become colloquially known, led westward from the Saltmarket and was also once a place of high note. It contained the mansions of several noble families, the original city bank, the Merchants' Hall, and the Assembly Rooms. Like the Saltmarket, the area became home to many merchants keen to cash in on new commodities and goods reaching Glasgow from trading ports abroad. The Briggait was a lively place, full of taverns, tenements and small shops jostling for space along the narrow alleyways, small lanes and streets. The area was known for its small eating-houses selling tripe and potted meats. Even the most fashionable families would send out staff to collect fresh supplies of this seventeenth-century delicacy. Located in the centre of the Briggait, Aird's Wynd was known as the gathering place where people could learn the news of the day and of events abroad.

right
The old Tolbooth.

The COLLEDGE of GLASGOW

Glasgow's great fires

The year 1666 is famous for the fire that swept across London, but Glasgow had its own great fire 14 years earlier, in June 1652. It started on the High Street, in the house of James Hamilton, and was swept along by a strong northwest wind. It soon reached the main crossroads where it spread south to the Saltmarket and east and west along Trongate and Gallowgate. Completely out of control, it reached as far south as the Bridgegate and it took 18 hours before the flames began to die down. By that time, a third of the city had been destroyed; the Town Council reported that 'thair will be neir four scoir closses all burnt, estimat about ane thousand families'. The buildings in this part of the town were made of timber and thatch and were very close together, which made the fire impossible to control.

Following the fire, the Council made great efforts to improve the cityscape and the surrounding environment, discouraging wooden and thatch construction of buildings and opening new water wells. This did not stop another fire breaking out in High Street in 1677, only this time it was caused by arson. A disgruntled blacksmith's apprentice, enraged by continual beatings from his master, set fire to the workshop. Unfortunately, he also burned down over 130 homes in the High Street. New laws were passed demanding that any new building should be built of stone and slate and that dangerous trades, such as candle making, be removed to beyond the city boundaries.
The city recovered valiantly from the disasters, and in 1715 the writer Daniel Defoe visited Glasgow and remarked that it was 'one of the cleanest, most beautiful and best built cities in Britain'.

left
View of the University of Glasgow and Blackfriar's Church, 1693.

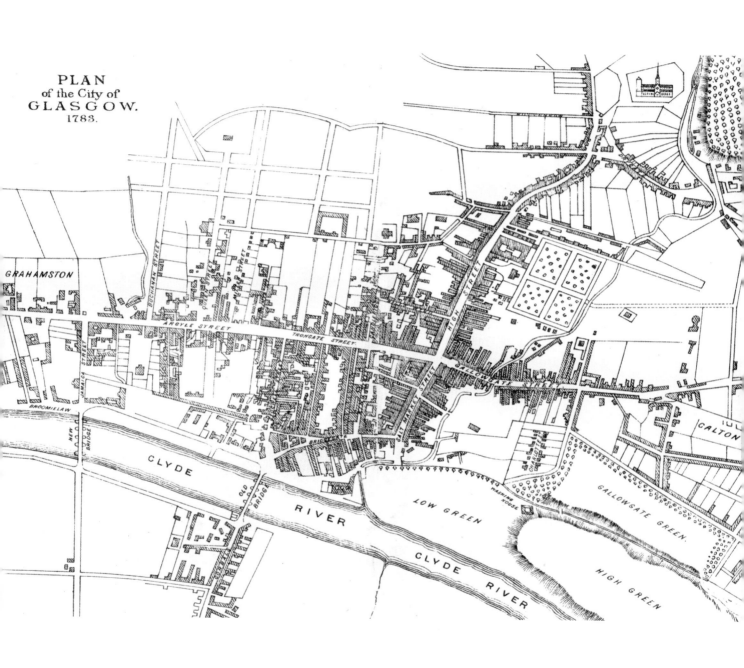

PLAN
of the City of
GLASGOW.
1783.

GRAHAMSTON

BUCHANAN STREET

ARGYLE STREET

TRONGATE STREET

HIGH STREET

GALLOWGATE STREET

SALT MARKET STREET

JAMAICA STREET

BROOMIELAW

NEW BRIDGE

OLD BRIDGE

CLYDE   RIVER

CLYDE   RIVER

LOW GREEN

WASHING HOUSE

CHARLOTTE STREET

CALTON

GALLOWGATE GREEN

HIGH GREEN

34

GLASGOW'S EXPANSION

Glasgow – Second City of the Empire

By the 1770s, Glasgow's population had reached 60,000 and the transformation of the city from ecclesiastical centre to mercantile hub was almost complete. Glasgow began to take advantage of its favourable westerly location and developed links with the British colonies in the West Indies for sugar and in America for tobacco.

The merchant classes sought to display their new wealth and status and escape the confines of the old medieval closes around the High Street and Saltmarket, which were becoming crowded and were unhealthy. New suburbs such as Queen Street, Buchanan Street and Jamaica Street were opened out to the west of the old town. The Trongate, once part of the periphery of the city, became Glasgow's 'Royal Mile', the administrative, commercial and cultural heart of the city and the scene of vast public meetings.

In 1787, Nathaniel Jones published his first Directory, describing the state of Glasgow and its citizens. While the city was undoubtedly growing, the sites of Laurieston, Tradeston, and Bridgeton, now a part of the inner city, were still cornfields or kitchen gardens. On Blythswood Hill, known in modern times as the central business district of Glasgow, country pursuits were followed and hares and partridges were often hunted for sport.

Left
Map of Glasgow, 1783, by James Lumsden.

The city's increasing wealth helped to develop trade and manufacturing and Glasgow's cottage industries developed into formalized factories, producing manufactured goods to be exported to new markets. By 1750, there were many factories producing a wide range of products, including linen, soap and refined sugar. In the business parts of the city, gilded signboards depicting golden fleeces, fish, boots and breeches swung in midair above lavishly decorated shops.

Until late in the eighteenth century, children could safely wade across the River Clyde at low water. The river was too shallow for most trading vessels and cargoes had to be unloaded and shipped up to the city river banks by small craft. However by 1770, the river had been dredged to increase its depth to 2.3 metres (7 feet 8 inches), allowing boats to navigate all the way to Glasgow Bridge. Glasgow now developed as a major port, overtaking Liverpool, Bristol and Whitehaven in importance. So great was Glasgow's success, that the City Fathers of these English ports complained to Parliament. From the economic standpoint, Glasgow was now thriving as never before and was recognized as a major centre of international trade.

In the years between 1780 and 1850, the population of Glasgow increased almost tenfold from 43,000 to 359,000. Glasgow had emerged as Scotland's largest city and as the centre of the cotton industry, steam locomotion and shipbuilding. It was now the Second City of the British Empire.

The changing faces of Provand's Lordship

In 1736 John M'Ure published the first history of the city of Glasgow. At this time Glasgow's population was around 15,000 people living in ten streets and 17 lanes, and on an area of ground approximately two square kilometres (three-quarters of a square mile) in extent. M'Ure's wrote enthusiastically about the city saying, 'It is the most beautiful city in the world for its bigness, and is acknowledged to be so by all foreigners that come thither.'

This same year, the title deeds of Provand's Lordship show that the house belonged to Mr Bryson of Neilsland. It is quite likely that this man had inherited the house from William Bryson, the tailor, who may have been his father or uncle. From Mr Bryson of Neilsland, the house travelled through three more generations of the family until 1753, when it became the property of Matthew Whitelaw, described as a maltman. In the property title the house is described as 'a great tenement of land' with 'stables, brewhouse, cellars, closs and pertinents'. Also mentioned for the first time is a little fore house and shop attached to the south side of the building, owned by a gentleman named Euphan Machen. In 1784, this small lean-to, since demolished, acquired a rather gruesome connection as the abode of the city executioner.

The earliest known place of public execution in Glasgow was east of the Gallowgate, outside the city walls, but in 1784, the gallows was moved for storage purposes to the cathedral and the execution site became the yard of the archbishop's castle. In the years between 1784 and 1787, ten men and two women suffered the ultimate penalty of death, only one of them having been found guilty of murder. The others were guilty of forgery, robbery, housebreaking and theft. On the occasion of an execution, the criminal was escorted out from the Tolbooth at Glasgow Cross, clothed in a loose dress of white linen with trimmings of black. The unfortunate prisoner was then led behind a cart carrying the coffin that would later be used for their body. Accompanied by the magistrates, town officers and a clergyman encouraging the individual with devotions and prayer, the procession slowly made its way up towards the cathedral. Every window lining the route up the High Street would be crowded with spectators watching this grisly episode. On arrival at the almshouse of St Nicholas' Hospital next to Provand's Lordship, the group would come to a standstill. The first verse of a psalm was sung, led by the condemned prisoner, and the mournful tones of the almshouse bell would ring to signal the granting of a last speech.

The bodies of the recently executed were buried in the common ground to the north of the cathedral, alongside the unbaptized and lunatics of the parish. A reminder of this can still be seen today in the form of a figure of a man dangling in a noose from a gibbet, cut deeply into a buttress on the north wall of the cathedral.

right
Castle Street looking north-east towards Glasgow Cathedral, early 1800s.

Castle St & Square Tower of Cathedral

39

Old Houses in Castle Street, opposite the Cathedral 1848.   Wm Simpson A

Provand's in the nineteenth century

Provand's Lordship, meanwhile, passed through a variety of hands. In 1814, the property passed to Robert McAlpen and John Wilson who appear to have rented at least some of the rooms to tenants. From 1842 to 1856, it was partially occupied by Mrs A Dudgeon, the proprietor of an alehouse. A large painting on leather by her son, artist Thomas Dudgeon, hung on the east wall as a tavern signboard for many years. It depicted the legendary battle of the Bell of the Brae, where Wallace defeated the English, and is now part of the Provand's Lordship collection held in store. Mrs Dudgeon's establishment was well known and on Sundays many people were known to visit after attending the service at the Barony Church opposite. There is a tradition that one farmer found himself so happy there that he remained in the alehouse all week and was surprised to find another Sunday arrive before his revelling was finished!

In 1854, Matthew Turnbull, a pattern drawer in Glasgow, purchased half of the building from McAlpen's trustees for £125. He married a daughter of John Wilson and Provand's Lordship was reunited as one dwelling.

left
Old Houses in Castle Street, opposite the cathedral, 1843, by William 'Crimea' Simpson.

right
Close no. 118 High Street.

Demolition and improvement

As the city expanded, Glasgow attracted a large number of immigrants seeking work, in particular from the Northern Highlands and Ireland. The incredible growth of the city brought with it the inevitable problems of slums and disease. The worst affected areas were around the old Glasgow Cross and High Street, where poor sanitation created high mortality rates through infection and disease. In 1842, an epidemic of cholera killed more than 4,000 people and further outbreaks of disease in 1848 and 1853 galvanized the City Corporation into action. They demolished parts of the Trongate, Gallowgate, Saltmarket and many of the buildings around the High Street where it was estimated that as many as 1,000 people resided in just one acre of slum-ridden tenement housing. Although the City Corporation professed to have only humanitarian motives, one contemporary report states that: 'Hoardes of the criminal classes sheltered in the dens and caverns of dwelling houses in the narrow lanes and dark closes, rendering the localities notorious in the annals of robbery and murder.'

The City Improvement Trust was created in 1866 to coordinate a programme of slum clearance and reconstruction. The university, once so admired on the High Street, had become surrounded by rundown vennels and lanes and in 1870, after complaints from the staff and students, a decision was taken to move the university to the cleaner and fresher air of the suburban outskirts of Glasgow. The old university buildings, including its chapel and celebrated botanical gardens, were demolished to make way for railway development.

Remodelling the cathedral precinct

The area around the cathedral and Provand's Lordship also suffered greatly from the zealous activities of the City Fathers and few of the old medieval buildings survived the Victorian obsession with 'Improvement'.

By the mid-nineteeth century, many of the prebendal manses had disappeared and the others were almost all in ruins. At this time, Provand's Lordship still had its crow step on the north gable of the building but this was destroyed in the mid-1840s when a new block of tenement housing was built on the site of the prebendal manse of Govan, adjacent to Provand's Lordship. The Manse of Renfrew, which stood on the north side of the Govan Manse, was also demolished. This building was the birthplace in 1804 of the distinguished watercolour artist, William Leighton Leitch. From his humble beginnings, Leitch rose to become drawing master to Queen Victoria and the Royal Family for 22 years. He said of the neighbourhood, 'it was a place endeared to me by a thousand happy memories, as it was here I was born and bred, and lived until I was nineteen years of age'. Referring to Provand's Lordship, he says:

> ... the big house on the left was called the Black Land. It was a heavy building, with a singular very wide stone staircase, which led up to the different storeys, very gloomy, with hardly any light, and the rooms large, gaunt and strangely proportioned. I recollect my father saying that he believed the house was called the Black Land from its having been the residence of some of the superior orders of the priesthood in the old times.

On the south side of Provand's Lordship, the last ruins of the hall and chapel of St Nicholas' Hospital had been removed in 1805 to open up Macleod Street and provide a route to Duke Street prison.

The earliest bridewell, or prison, in Glasgow was an old building on the south side of the Drygate, which had formerly been the manse of the Prebend of Cambuslang. In 1635, the property was gifted to the city magistrates by the then owner, the Earl of Glencairn, and was converted into 'a house of correction, for the confinement of vagrants and dissolute women'. By 1789, this building was no longer sufficient for the growing population and by

1798 the City magistrates had secured more suitable premises on Duke Street. The original prison building had six storeys and contained 115 cells, and during the nineteenth century it was extended to become a model of the Victorian penal workhouse. Inmates were encouraged to engage in useful industry, from weaving to cabinet making. However, between the years 1865 and 1928, a number of prisoners were executed here in the grounds. The prison staff prevented onlookers by shielding the executions with white sheets. Duke Street prison was finally closed in 1955. The site is now a housing scheme with the only surviving element of the gaol being part of the perimeter wall.

Behind the cathedral on Fir Park, the Necropolis was the first planned cemetery in the city and was designed to provide a suitable resting place for the wealthy classes of Victorian Glasgow. The genteel middle classes wished to protect themselves from horrific epidemics of cholera and typhoid in the lower town and avoid burying family members in the overcrowded churchyards where the 'stench emitted in hot weather was insufferable'.
The location high above the city provided an appropriate resting place for the city's great and good. In common with other Victorian cemeteries, the Necropolis was designed as a botanic and sculpture garden and was non-denominational. The foundation stone of the John Knox statue was laid in 1825 and almost every eminent Glaswegian who died between 1832 and 1867 is recorded among the tombs and cenotaphs.

right
Glasgow Necropolis and
statue of John Knox in the
background.

This period of demolition and 'improvement' was not just about getting rid of unhealthy housing; it had begun much earlier and represented something deeper in the psyche of Glasgow and its people.

Over the previous two centuries, the bishop's castle had gradually fallen into disrepair, but calculated demolition of the bishop's castle only began after the city magistrates gave permission for stone to be used in the building of a new inn, Saracen's Head, still open in Duke Street. When the Royal Infirmary was founded in 1789, the last relics of the castle were removed to clear the site and some of the stones were used in the new building. The last glimpse of the castle is found in Lettice's *Tour of Scotland* (1794), where the following passage occurs:

> We saw workmen very busy in pulling down a grand ruin near the cathedral, the remains of the Episcopal Palace. But this will occasion you no surprise, as every body knows how little partiality the inhabitants of North Britain entertain for the Episcopal order and all its appendages.

St Mungo Museum now stands on the site of the bishop's castle but little except the street name, Castle Street, remains as a reminder of the area's glorious past. In 1840, it was decided that the cathedral would be visually improved if the two western towers were demolished and new towers constructed. Despite a few voices of discontent, a bell tower and consistory court were demolished.

These new towers were never built and further plans
to embellish the cathedral with mock-gothic pinnacles
and turrets were also fortunately shelved. The demolition
of the cathedral epitomized the work of the City
Improvement Trust. While the Trust did much good work
in improving sanitation and the health and wellbeing of
Glaswegians, it also engaged in wholesale destruction of
what remained of the medieval city.

right
Ruins of bishop's castle and
cathedral towers.

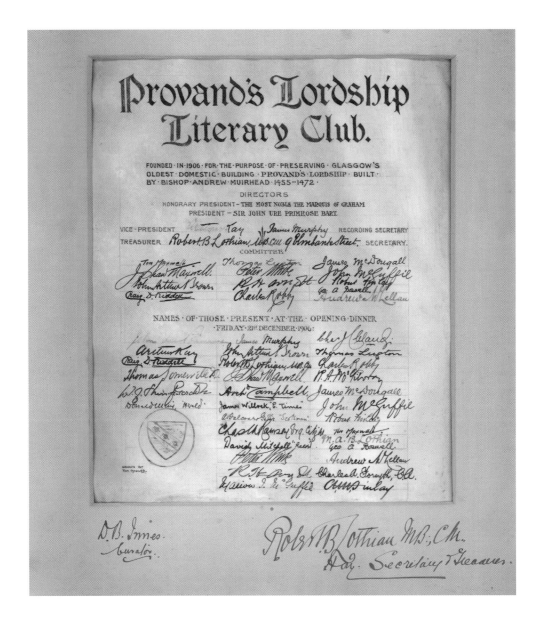

RESCUING GLASGOW'S PAST

The Provand's Lordship Society

In 1904, plans were proposed to extend the Royal Infirmary and it seemed likely that Provand's Lordship would be threatened with destruction. By this time, the house had been subdivided into three shops, a barber, a greengrocer and a sweet shop. The Provand's Lordship Society was formed by a group of men and women committed to saving the house and developing it as a centre of archaeological, literary and artistic life. Many prominent citizens of the city attended their foundation dinner.

Parts of the building were opened to the public in 1908 and a series of fund-raising exhibitions helped to finance the acquisition of the property. In the early days, the Society met in the house and entered through the sweet shop, owned at the time by a Mr W Innes. The members would climb up a small ladder to reach the two rooms allocated for Society purposes.

Early in 1927, the Society enlisted the help of Sir William Burrell, Glasgow shipping agent and philanthropist. He established a fund to acquire objects to furnish the house and recreate the interior as it might have been around 1700.

left
Memento from the inauguration dinner of the Provand's Lordship Society.

Isaac Morton and family

Isaac Morton and his family were the last tenants of Provand's Lordship. Jane and Isaac Morton ran a small factory producing aerated water and a sweet shop with refreshment room, both on the ground floor. Sweets and boilings were made on the premises, and the machines used by the Morton family for making toffee balls, acid drops, and pan drops can still be seen on the ground floor of Provand's Lordship.

The Morton family gave up their premises after World War I and the building was handed over to the Provand's Lordship Society.

above
The Morton family, last residents of Provand's Lordship.

left
Sweetshop display, ground floor of Provand's Lordship.

opposite
Provand's Lordship, 1903.

The Provand's Lordship collection

With the assistance of Sir William Burrell, the original Provand's Lordship Society members collected many of the objects on display in the house today. As the Society developed, local citizens of Glasgow also donated objects such as the household implements and pewter in the kitchen area.

Thanks to Burrell's support, Provand's Lordship also holds one of the most important collections of early Scottish chairs. Until the seventeenth century, chairs were not commonplace and were therefore symbols of wealth and authority. The skill and materials needed to create even the simplest of chairs meant they were a symbol of influence and power.

Many of the chairs in the Provand's Lordship collection are described as 'Aberdeen' chairs. Most were made in the north-east of Scotland and derive from the 'caqueteuse' style, favoured by the French. Also known as the 'gossips' chair, the design is high and narrow in the back, with splayed armrests and footrest, allowing those in conversation to exchange quiet confidences. One of the earliest chairs is located in the mid-chamber of the first floor and comes from the House of Kelly, Aberdeenshire. Closely modelled on the French 'caqueteuse' style, the chair is inscribed with the initials G and I and is dated 1582.

left
Display of pewter, ground floor of Provand's Lordship.

right
House of Kelly chair, dated
1582.

right
Chalmers and Forbes
marriage chair.

Many of the chairs in the collection are inscribed and dated, and have a very special significance. They are known as marriage chairs and record the marriage date, the initials of the partners and often a coat of arms. These chairs are tangible marriage records of the seventeenth and eighteenth century, lasting public displays of the union of two families. One of these marriage chairs is on display on the first floor in the southwest room. The chair is dated 1667 and is inscribed with the initials 'WMC' for William Chalmers, Professor of Divinity at Aberdeen University, and 'IF' for Isabella Forbes, his wife, and is carved with their joint coat of arms.

Also of particular interest are the various stained-glass panelsfitted into the windows of the first floor, acquired with monies from Sir William Burrell's fund. The large stained-glass panel in the east window of the southern room shows the coat of arms of Sir Francis Wortley, a knight and baronet of the seventeenth century. Sir Francis Wortley was created a baronet by King James I and VI, and took sides with the Royalists in the English Civil War of 1642–48. He recruited 600 troops and turned his home, Wortley Hall, into a fortress. Sir Francis Wortley commanded his garrison of soldiers at Tankersley Moor, in Yorkshire, where he was captured by the Roundheads and imprisoned in the Tower of London. He is remembered for writing popular songs and ballads supporting the Royalist cause.

Many of the other panels on display are small sections of medieval glass, remodelled in the eighteenth century to create interesting and decorative panels for wealthy households.

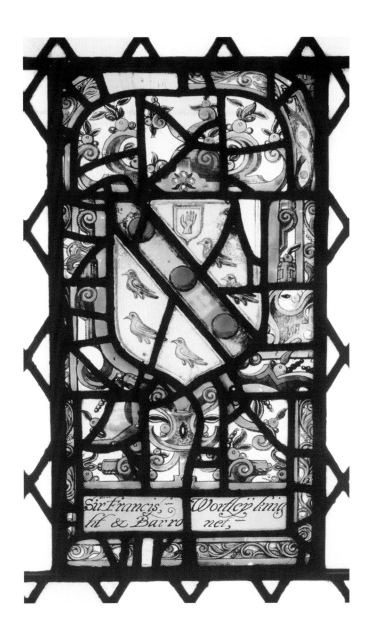

right
Stained glass panel
depicting the arms of Sir
Francis Wortley, baronet
and knight.

Sir William Burrell

Sir William Burrell was born on 9 July 1861, the third of nine children. Even as a child, he was a passionate collector and often spent his pocket money on paintings and curios.

The Burrell family were shipping agents and in 1875 William followed in the footsteps of his father and grandfather and entered the family firm. His business trips abroad allowed him to gain a wider knowledge of the art world, and to collect works that interested him. Burrell learnt the skills necessary to land a bargain and earned him enough money to invest in his passion for collecting.

At the age of 40 he married Constance Mitchell, daughter of another ship-owner and the following year, with the birth of a daughter, the family moved to a large house on Great Western Road.

Burrell had eclectic tastes and travelled widely to build up an important collection ranging from Chinese ceramics to stained glass and in 1927 he was knighted for his public work and services to art.

In 1944, he gave almost his entire collection to the City of Glasgow and in 1983 Glasgow City Council opened the Burrell Collection, a purpose-built home for the collection, open free of charge to the public.

Sir William Burrell took an active interest in Provand's Lordship and is responsible for acquiring much of the collection displayed today. Despite being described as more interested in foreign works, the collection at Provand's Lordship is testimony to Sir William Burrell's interest in Scotland's medieval past.

Sir William Burrell at about the age of 60.

ST NICHOLAS GARDEN

Most of the prebendal houses and manses in medieval Glasgow had gardens and orchards but over the centuries these have all but disappeared. The Garden of St Nicholas, behind Provand's Lordship, was designed in 1995 by Gary Johnson for the architects James Cunning Young & Partners as part of a competition to provide a lasting memory of the original fifteenth-century garden that once stood behind Provand's Lordship.

The garden recreates the atmosphere of a traditional physic garden of the late medieval and early Renaissance period in Glasgow, when gardens were designed to grow plants and herbs for medicinal and culinary purposes. Each flowerbed in the St Nicholas Garden contains plants with particular qualities to relieve certain ailments. The garden is grown with box hedging and is designed around a Celtic knot design. At the centre is a water fountain, intended as a focal point for contemplation.

Medieval physic gardens in Glasgow

In the late fifteenth century most hospitals and infirmaries had gardens that provided plants for the relief and refreshment of the poor, and St Nicholas' Hospital was no exception. Herbs, fruits and other plants were used in cooking and for the preparation of medicines, medicinal baths and for other health-giving purposes, including the production of scented candles for dispelling disease.

left
St Nicholas Garden,
October 2003.

There are known to have been at least two other physic gardens in the area between 1500 and 1700. The first of these gardens is recorded in 1555 and is linked to Mark Jameson, a member of the Vicars Choral at Glasgow Cathedral, the cathedral choir first established by Bishop Andrew Muirhead a hundred years previously. He was also Deputy Rector of Glasgow University and benefactor of St Nicholas Hospital. It is not known exactly where his garden was, but it may well have been located at his residence behind the cathedral.

Another physic garden was located on the High Street, within the grounds of the old Glasgow University and dates from 1740. It is described as:

> … a large fine Garden, with broad pleasant walks, for the use of Masters and Students to walk in, consisting of seven Acres of ground, well furnished with Fruit Trees and Pot herbs; as like wise a Physic-Garden of a Rood of Ground, well fenced about with a strong high Stone Wall.

This great garden is commemorated today by the planting of the cherry orchard to the west of St Nicholas Garden, which pays tribute to the 'great orchard' of the old medieval university.

right
North end of the college garden and cathedral spire. Engraving by Robert Paul, 1762.

A View of the Middle Walk in the College-garden.
Academy Glasgow. 1762.

Rob. Paul sc.

Medieval medicine

Medical care in the medieval period involved a wide variety of techniques including 'holistic' diets, bloodletting and the use of holy relics, prayers and other ritual acts. The theory of humours, from the Greek and Roman periods, was important to medieval practitioners. It was based around the idea that the human body contained four fluids called humours: blood, phlegm, yellow bile and black bile. It was thought that the excess of one fluid caused disease, and herbs were used to rebalance the body. Medieval doctors also favoured the 'Doctrine of Signatures'. This method centred on the idea that the appearance of a plant showed its uses. Consequently, a plant like heartsease, or sweet violet, with its small heart shaped leaves, would assist in treating a heart complaint. 'Acts of virtue', such as prayers to saints, charity and pilgrimages were also vitally important, as medicine was closely linked with religion. Medieval practitioners used herbs and plants in drinks, pills, ointments, baths, poultices, and many other imaginative forms to treat illness.

Medieval and Renaissance gardens

Medieval and particularly Renaissance gardening was heavily influenced by the writings of the ancient Greeks and Romans and gardens were intended not only as a delight to the senses, but also as areas to produce food and medicines. Trees were planted either along walls or geometrically placed in orchards. Some trees, such as the walnut, were avoided in gardens, but fruit trees and other trees with a good smell or pleasant aspect were included in most gardens as well as adjoining orchards. Water features were very important in gardens of this period and fountains and pools were included from which water could be drawn or washing done. Covered walks, like cloisters, gave people an area to walk or relax and shelter from the rain. Most manors, abbeys, and great estates would have utilitarian gardens, farm fields, and perhaps vineyards or orchards in addition to some sort of pleasure garden.

St Nicholas

According to tradition, Nicholas of Bari was born into a noble family in the fourth century and became the bishop of the Christian Church in the city of Myra, in modern-day Turkey. Nicholas performed many astonishing miracles both before and after his death, guaranteeing his sainthood. For example, he miraculously supplied grain for the starving during a famine and is also credited with restoring to life three boys who had been chopped up and pickled in salt by a butcher.

Saints were widely venerated in the medieval world and Nicholas was regarded with particular devotion in Scotland, where he became the patron saint of Aberdeen. Chapels, gardens and hospitals were dedicated to his name and feasts were celebrated on 6 December, his festival day. In Glasgow, an early chapel to St Nicholas stood on the north side of Gallowgate, near the Molendinar Burn. Later, Andrew Muirhead built the Hospital and Chapel of St Nicholas in honour of the saint's work with the poor.

There are numerous legends associated with the life of St Nicholas, many related to his works of charity. One story tells of a nobleman in Myra who was so poor he could not afford to provide a dowry for his three daughters. To save them from shame and starvation, St Nicholas left a bag of gold inside their window on three successive nights and with this, the daughters were able to marry. St Nicholas was, therefore, not only a friend to the poor but also the bringer of gifts. The three bags of gold are still today symbolized in the three golden balls of pawnbrokers' signs. Many European children still receive gifts on St Nicholas Day, but in Britain, St Nicholas has become the Father Christmas of 25 December.

Stained glass panel
depicting St Nicholas,
the Burrell Collection,
Glasgow.

TONTINE FACES

The origins of the Tontine Faces

Enclosing the Garden of St Nicholas is a cloistered walkway and set within each bay is an intriguing carved face. These strange masks are known collectively as the 'Tontine Faces', a unique part of Glasgow's history with an interesting story to tell.

The story of the Tontine Faces begins in 1736, with the erection of a new town hall at Glasgow Cross. The building, opened in 1740, had a superb piazza frontage of five archways, into which master stonemason David Cation carved five stone faces as keystones. The building was extended in 1758, and five more bays were added with additional faces carved by Cation's colleague Mungo Naismith. In front of the Tontine Hotel stood a statue depicting King William III of Orange astride a stately horse, presented to the City in 1734 by James MacRae, Governor of the Presidency of Madras. The statue commemorates the accession to the throne of Protestant 'King Billy' in 1689, and now stands in the small park just to the south of Provand's Lordship.

In 1781, the building was acquired by the Tontine Society and re-opened as the Tontine Hotel and Coffee Room. The building took its name from Lorenzo Tonti, an Italian advisor to the French court. In 1653, he started a scheme

left
The Trongate, Glasgow, also known as *Old Glasgow Cross,* 1826, by John Knox. The Tontine Hotel and statue of King William can be seen in the centre of the painting.

whereby subscribers paid a sum into a fund, and in return received dividends from the capital invested. As each person died the individual's share was divided among all the others until only one was left, reaping all the benefits. By the eighteenth century, Glasgow had a thriving Tontine Society boasting many illustrious members. Tontines were eventually banned in Britain because there was too much incentive for subscribers to 'dispose' of each other to increase their share of the fund, or to become the last survivor and so claim the capital!

The Tontine Hotel and Coffee House, with its unusual carved keystones, became one of the best-known architectural features of the city and the main haunt of Glasgow's famous Tobacco Lords. These men were some of the great innovators of capitalism in the 1700s and were making vast sums of money from their business ventures in America. As their tobacco plantations expanded and they cornered the market from Glasgow's advantageous location on the west coast, Glasgow's Tobacco Lords became Scotland's first millionaires. Their legacy can be seen in the street names in the city centre. Ingram Street, Buchanan Street, Glassford Street and Virginia Street all take their names from prominent Glasgow merchants. These men would meet at the front of the Tontine Building and the coffee room under the piazza. No tradesman or shopkeeper dared to address them in an off-hand way, or intrude upon the promenade ground, under pain of the highest displeasure. A later account gives a picturesque description of successful merchants at this time:

They assumed important airs and the deportment of very superior persons, looking down upon their fellow tradesmen and dependants with a superciliousness that would be laughed at in these days. They considered themselves princes, and strutted about on the Plainstanes as if they were the rulers of the destinies of Glasgow. They were like the merchants of Venice distinguished by a particular garb, being attired in scarlet cloaks, curled wigs, cocked hats, and bearing gold-headed canes.

The travels of the Tontine Faces

In 1869, the Tontine Hotel was converted into a drapers shop and renovations were proposed for the building, which included the demolition of the lower arcade holding the ten Tontine Faces. The faces had become a focal point of the street landscape and their removal caused huge uproar among local people. In his 1872 guide to Glasgow, John Tweed lamented the loss of the Tontine Building: '… alas! Transformed into a drapery warehouse … The beauty of the Tontine has disappeared; even the sculptured masks which stretched along the whole front have vanished.'

The ten masks were removed and acquired by the Glasgow builder Peter Shannan who was building a new warehouse for Messrs Fraser Sons & Co at the bottom of Buchanan Street. This new building had 13 bays and so he used the ten original 'Tontine' masks and added a further three, carved in a similar style by his sculptor son Archibald Macfarlane Shannan. They stayed there until 1888, when the building was burnt down. At this point, the faces were removed and disappeared into obscurity. However, thanks to a concerted campaign by Glasgow journalist James Cowan, whose pseudonym was 'Peter Prowler', the Tontine Faces were tracked down to various sites around the city and were finally reunited in 1995, when the St Nicholas Garden was opened. Of the ten original Tontine Faces, only nine are on display in the garden; the last one, one of the five 'theatrical' masks has never been recovered. Two of the carvings are the work of Archibald Macfarlane Shannon and the remaining two carvings are more modern and only loosely connected with the originals, having been part of a separate scheme on the Frasers building.

The Tontine Faces hold a unique place in Glasgow's history and folklore and there is a well-established custom among Glasgow parents to caution sulking children not to 'make a Tontine Face'. In his work, *Glasgow and its Clubs,* written in 1864, John Strang describes the Tontine Faces as 'caricature countenances which so long excited wonder and laughter among crowds of gaping gossipers'. It is fitting therefore, that these wonderful and intriguing grotesque carved faces should find a final home in the grounds of Glasgow's oldest house.

right
Tontine Faces. The nine original Tontine Faces are on display in the St Nicholas Garden.

John Glassford – tobacco lord

Born in 1715, John Glassford is remembered as one of Glasgow's most famous tobacco lords. A great businessman and trader, the novelist Tobias Smollett described him as 'one of the greatest merchants in Europe'.

In 1750, following success in other business ventures, John Glassford began trading in the new and lucrative commodity of tobacco. He quickly built up a fleet of 25 vessels and developed a successful string of stores across the state of New England, America. Like other tobacco merchants, John Glassford began to diversify and became involved in dye making and the textile industry. He also developed an interest in banking, and helped to establish the successful Thistle Bank in 1761. As a member of the great and good of Glasgow, John Glassford was a prominent member of the Tontine Society and often took coffee in the Tontine Coffee House.

He was a great landowner and owned property in Ayrshire and Lanarkshire. His country house was located at Douglaston, north of Glasgow, and he spent much time and money on developing the fields into beautiful gardens.

The setting for his family portrait was the Shawfield Mansion, Glasgow's most splendid townhouse, just off the Trongate in what is now Glassford Street. The rich carpet and fine clothes show the family's wealth and influence. The painting also originally showed a black manservant standing behind John Glassford. In the eighteenth century many wealthy Glaswegians showed their status by bringing black servants from the slave plantations of the West Indies to serve in their homes. However, the slave was subsequently painted out in the nineteenth century, due to the influence of the growing anti-slavery movement.

John Glassford & Family, c.1767, by Archibald McLauchlan.

THE RECENT HISTORY OF PROVAND'S LORDSHIP

Glasgow Museums' involvement

In 1978, facing the prospect of extensive and costly repairs, the Provand's Lordship Society offered the building to Glasgow District Council. In 1925, work had been undertaken to tie in the east wall, which was beginning to bulge. The brick chimneys were removed and replaced by stone and the beams and flooring were renovated and treated for rot and woodworm. In 1976, issues around the fabric of Provand's Lordship were raised again but the Society was unable to finance the work needed and approached Glasgow District Council. The building was restored with the generous assistance of Frank Lafferty, a local builder, who completed the work for the sum of one new penny. A steel frame was constructed in the roof space and as grant monies became available, the walls were stitched with steel rods. In order to preserve the original fifteenth-century oak floor beams, false floors were introduced on the upper floors, which have protected the floors but unfortunately altered the proportions of some of the rooms and fireplaces. When the tenement adjoining Provand's Lordship was demolished in the 1980s, a new masonry outer skin was constructed and the external walls were washed and repointed. The building is now a Grade A Listed Building, demanding that all major repairs and conservation work are subject to approval by Historic Scotland. More recently, conservation and restoration work has been carried out on the southwest gable, funded by the City with support from Historic Scotland. Over recent years, a number of archaeological projects have been undertaken to gain a greater understanding of the area, including the excavation of the foundations of the bishop's castle. Work continues to preserve Provand's Lordship and the surrounding area and to protect the remaining buildings against the pressures of modern environmental conditions.

right
Foundations of the bishop's castle exposed during archaeological excavations, 1991.

Educational activities and family events

Provand's Lordship has a dedicated team of staff who continue to care for the building and to develop new resources for visitors to Glasgow's oldest house. The Education team welcomes schools, families and members of the public to explore the history of Provand's Lordship through costume and handling object boxes, and brings the history of Glasgow alive with workshops, talks and events.

Provand's Lordship today

Today, Provand's Lordship provides a unique opportunity to step back in time and explore some of Glasgow's lost history. Glasgow's oldest house has seen times of intrigue, treachery, turmoil and progress, and stands witness to the city's colourful and exciting past.

right
School workshop in progress at Provand's Lordship.

TIMELINE

c.600: St Mungo establishes a Christian site on the banks of the Molendinar.

1136: King David I attends the blessing of Glasgow's first stone church.

1175: Glasgow is granted a Burgh Charter.

1450: Glasgow becomes a Burgh of Regality.

1451: The University of Glasgow is founded by Bishop Turnbull.

1471: Bishop Andrew Muirhead builds Provand's Lordship.

1492: Robert Blacader is elected first Archbishop of Glasgow.

1560: The Protestant Reformation reaches Glasgow. James Beaton, Glasgow's last Catholic bishop, is forced to flee to France.

1603: James VI of Scotland becomes James I of England, bringing about the Union of the Crowns.

1652: Nearly one third of the city is destroyed by fire.

1677: A second great fire hits Glasgow.

1707: Scotland and England are formally united to form Great Britain in the Act of Union. This allows Glasgow greater trading freedoms.

1770: The River Clyde is deepened, establishing Glasgow as a deep-water port.

1789: Glasgow Royal Infirmary founded.

1794: Robert Adam builds the Trades House in Glassford Street. The 14 trades represented are: bakers, barbers, coopers, cordiners, dyers, fleshers, gardeners, hammermen, maltmen, masons, skinners, tailors, weavers and wrights.

1811: Glasgow is recognized as the largest city in Scotland and the second city of the British Empire.

1818: Typhus epidemic.

1848: A cholera epidemic spreads across Glasgow causing many deaths.

1860: Glasgow receives a fresh water supply from Loch Katrine.

1870: The University of Glasgow moves to the cleaner air of Gilmorehill in the West End.

1888: Glasgow's first International Exhibition opens.

1896: Glasgow School of Art is designed by Charles Rennie Mackintosh.

1901: Glasgow Museum and Art Gallery is opened at Kelvingrove Park.

1906: Provand's Lordship Society is established.

1979: Glasgow City Council accepts care of Provand's Lordship.

1983: Glasgow City Council opens the Burrell Collection in the south of the city.

1988: Glasgow hosts the National Garden Festival, which attracts 4.3 million visitors.

1990: Glasgow is named European Capital of Culture, representing a new era for the city. The Royal Concert Hall is opened.

1993: Opening of St Mungo Museum of Religious Life and Art, built on the site of the bishop's castle.

1999: Glasgow is named the UK City of Architecture and Design and hosts a year-long festival.

2001: The University of Glasgow celebrates its 550th anniversary.

FURTHER READING

Boney, A.D. (1988). *The Lost Gardens of Glasgow University*, London: Christopher Helm.

Driscoll, S.T. (2002). *Excavations at Glasgow Cathedral 1988–1997*, London: Maney Publishing.

Foreman, C. (2001). *Hidden Glasgow*, Edinburgh: John Donald.

Foreman, C. (2002). *Lost Glasgow, Glasgow's Lost Architectural Heritage*, Edinburgh: Birlinn.

McKean, C., Walker, D. and Walker, F. (1993). *Central Glasgow: An Illustrated Architectural Guide*, Glasgow: Pillans & Wilson Ltd.

A number of publications that have been of great help in this publication are now out of print, but may be found in major reference libraries such as the Mitchell Library, Glasgow.

Cleland, J. (1817). *Annals of Glasgow*, Glasgow: Khull & Co.

Gordon, J.F.S. (Ed.) (1872). *Glasghu Facies: A View of the City of Glasgow*, Glasgow: John Tweed.

Lugton, T. (1910). *The Old Ludgings of Glasgow, pre-Reformation Manses etc.*, Glasgow: James Hedderwick.

Websites

www.glasgowmuseums.com
www.theglasgowstory.com